The Ultimate
Indian Cookbook

**Healthy and Quick Recipes for Every Day
incl. Vegan und Vegetarian Recipes**

1st Edition

Ashwin Atkinson

ISBN- 9781700439192

Table of Contents

Introduction

Indian food can mean so many different things to different people, depending on context and personal preference. Although Indian food is commonly regarded as spicy, those among us who do not appreciate fiery cuisine and tongue tingling curries can nevertheless enjoy an Indian meal without apprehension. Indian food is very much a cultural funfair, and it depends on where in India you find yourself, what your menu will present.

Firstly, do not fear the burn as I did on my first visit! Simply ask the chef to hold the chilies, and you're good to go if you are not a lover of spicy-hot fare. Vindaloo is possibly the hottest curry, best known on the Indian food menu, as is Chettinad cuisine, while Korma and pasanda are typically the mildest.

There is just too much to say on the subject of a guide to Indian food, so let's just touch on the basics. An Indian food guide must include the various constituents of a characteristic Indian meal, which may be grouped into:

- Indian bread: naan, chapati, roti, paratha, or idli
- Side dishes: salad, papad1, pickles
- Main dishes: meat and/or vegetables
- Rice
- Daal: lentil dish

Any guide to Indian food requires knowledge of how to eat these components. It is important to appreciate the uniqueness of each dish by sampling each separately. Dish up a little of each main dish and whatever you choose of the side dishes. With your right hand, pick up a little vegetable or meat with a smallish piece of Indian bread, fold the bread over the food and pop it into your mouth and follow up with finger food from a side dish. After you have finished

---

1   Papad/papadum is a thin, crisp, disc-shaped dough-based Indian side accompaniment, either fried or cooked with dry heat

the bread, start with the rice and a little daal, as the two are traditionally eaten together. Work the rice and main dish or rice and daal into a manageable sized ball with your fingers and flick it into your mouth using your thumb. This can be understandably messy once you have worked through the entire meal, and this is where you get to use the small bowl of water with the slice of lemon placed on the table for the purpose of cleaning the fingers.

It is customary for Indians to enjoy many small meals in a day. Typically, morning prayers are followed up with a light meal of hot chai and something salty to eat. Breakfast of traditional fried flat bread stuffed with potato, or *halwa*, or toasted bread and egg will be taken some hours after waking. The afternoon snack of *namkeen*, appetizers and snacks, is actually eaten in the early evening, at around 5 or 6. Namkeen may include *samosas*, *bhel phuri*, or fresh fruits such as pomegranate, mangoes or grapes. Dinner is served fairly late at night and constitutes more than one vegetable dish, rice, and chapati. Before retiring to bed a cup of hot milk steeped with cardamom with a dash of sugar is the norm. The midday is broken with workers or students enjoying a *tiffin*[2] from home, often filled with chapati, veg dishes and rice, and perhaps a fruit.

---

2 Tiffin is an Indian English word for a type of meal, midday luncheon or a snack, depending on the Indian region usage,

History

India as a region has a very long history and covers a very large geographic area, populated by a very diverse mix of people numbering over a billion. The population has been impacted by people of many cultures and countries over thousands of years. As such it can be expected that the diet and menu will be varied. Over its 8000 year history, India has seen the influence of many countries, cultures, and cuisines.

Religion also plays a role in Indian food and diet, and despite the country's many religions, two cultures dominate food habits and cooking in India: Hindu and Muslim. Hinduism as the dominant religion has contributed towards vegetarianism prevailing, together with its offshoot Jainism, because the belief prescribes respect for all life forms. Vegetarianism is especially prevalent in the North, leading to the main source of protein being not meat or fish but rather lentils and beans. In the Hindu belief, cows are seen as sacred, therefore any and all milk products are considered auspicious inclusions in the cuisine. These include vegan cottage cheese, curd, and sweets containing milk solids. Meat and fish were established with the establishment of Muslim rule in 1194 AD, bringing also rice, dates, nuts, and grilled meat kebabs. The gourmet meal rituals inherent to Muslim rulers became ensconced in Indian heritage, as is evident today.

While the many diverse settlers and invaders, notably the Portuguese, the Persians and the British, injected their unique culinary traditions and taste, the specialties and cooking methods from the Indian cuisine have been blended to perfection.

Hindu vegetarian tradition prevails while the non-vegan Muslim tradition is most evident in India's Mughlai cuisine brought to the country by the Persians and Moguls many moons ago. Mughlai's rogan josh, rich Kormas (curries), nargisi koftas (meatballs), biryani (rice and meat layers), and tandoor dishes are all thanks to India's Muslim settlers in India. While on matters of origins of particulars dishes, it is interesting to look closer at those with Persian and Afghani influences that are further embelished by the Mughals during their period of rule over the Indian subcontinent.

Let us then begin with Idli, the savoury rice cake made by steaming a batter consisting of fermented black lentils and rice. Although the origins are not definite, many speculations exist which can be visited. The Chinese chronicler Xuang Zang determined that India had no steaming vessels, and that these were introduced by those cooks accompanying the Hindu Kings of Indonesia between 800 and 1200 AD. Writings indicate, however, that Arab traders brought 'rice balls' to the southern belt of India when they married and settled here. These Arab settlers were strictly halaal neo-converts to Islam, and so reverted to the easily made and safe to eat rice balls. The 970 AD Kannada writing 'Vaddaradhane' complicates these suppositions by featuring Idli as among the eighteen dishes served to a visiting Brahmachari.

Since Idli and Sambar are inseparable, it must be assumed that Sambar was also around between 800 and 1200 AD. But no, this lentil-based vegetable stew cooked with tamarind broth only saw the light of Indian day in the 18th century. Shahuji, the Thanjavur Marathas ruler really enjoyed a dish known as amti, made special by kokum as a main ingredient. The supposition runs that when the court ran out of supplies of imported kokum, tamarind pulp was suggested as a substitute for the sour ingredient. Shahji served the experimental dish to his visiting cousin, Sambhaji. The well enjoyed dish was embraced and named after their guest, Sambhaji. The other theory is that Sambhaji, the son of a Maratha ruler tried his hand at daal during his chef's absence, adding tamarind which he dared to be corrected. The dare not taken up meant the tamarind remained as an accepted ingredient.

Biryani has its origin in the Persian word 'birian' meaning 'fried before cooking'. The legend goes to the era 1593 to 1631 when Sha Jahan's queen, Mumtaz Mahal felt that the soldiers in the army barracks she visited were under-nourished. She instructed a special dish of balanced nutrition be prepared. The biryani was the perfect complete meal, eaten as a single serving, with Persian and Afghani influence crafted by the Mughals. Another tale suggests its origins in the rice dish "Oon Soru" evident in Tamil in 2 AD. The dish to feed military warriors was comprised of rice, meat, ghee, pepper, coriander, turmeric, and bay leaf. Yet another involves Timur The Lame, a member of the Turkicized Barlas tribe, the Turkic is renowned over time for his barbarous conquests from India and Russia to the Mediterranean Sea. Timur's Mongol subgroup travelled from Kazakhstan to Northern India via Afghanistan, during which time nomads buried an earthen pot filled with rice, meat, rice and spices in a pit. When the concoction was retrieved, it was forever more to be known as biriyani.

Preparing the Kitchen

Indian food is inherently freshly prepared. That is what makes it so unique and healthy, and of course cost effective. It also gives the impression that Indian food takes a long time to prepare. While this may seem unavoidable, there are many steps one can take in preparing the kitchen for making Indian food even easier than it already is.

Ingredients common to most Indian dishes can be pre-prepared in advance to further reduce cooking time. And there are a good many of these common ingredients to be had, which should always be available in the kitchen if Indian fare is going to be a norm.

FRESH HERBS

Coriander, known in India as dhania, and mint are a must have to prepare fresh chutneys obligatory in Indian meals, to add to gravies and salads and for garnishing. Coriander and mint are really easy to grow at home, requiring very little space. They can even supply the kitchen from a pot in the kitchen window, in window boxes on a small veranda, balcony or patio, or as companion plants in your flower garden or kitchen garden.

SPICES

Getting around the Indian spices and seasonings for cooking can be quite intimidating as a beginner faced with the plentiful selection. To make this a little less daunting, concentrate rather on three tiers ranked by ease and frequency of use and availability. I won't include black pepper and salt in the lists, as this is more or less a given in any kitchen. Any kitchen involved in the production of Indian dishes will also always have fresh ginger, fresh garlic, fresh mint, and fresh cilantro or coriander (dhania).

BASIC SPICES

- Ground Cumin
- Ground Coriander
- Chili powder
- Cinnamon sticks
- Cayenne pepper
- Bay leaves
- Dried chilies
- Turmeric
- Nutmeg
- Mustard seeds
- Fennel seeds
- Cloves

DELUXE ASSORTMENT

- Cardamom pods
- Cumin seeds
- Coriander seeds
- Saffron
- Star anise
- Poppy seeds
- Dried coconut
- Moong dal (skinned split mung beans)
- Masoor dal (red split lentils)
- Split peas: chana dal, urad dal, toovar, and dal.
- Garam Masala: has as many variances as there are regions in India, but the basis can be simplified to a ratio of 3 parts cumin:2 parts coriander:1 part remaining ingredients which may be a mixture of these all ground up to store in an airtight container:
- Anise/Fennel seeds
- Black pepper
- Dry ground ginger

- Cardamom
- Cloves
- Cinnamon
- Bay leaves

SUPER DELUXE ASSORTMENT

- Fenugreek seeds
- Curry/kahri leaves. If you can't find this, feel free to use lime juice and fresh basil as an emergency substitute. Never try to replace with curry powder, which is not at all similar.
- Tamarind
- Asafoetida (Hing) may be substituted with garlic in an emergency.
- Jaggery is raw unrefined cane sugar and can, in an emergency, be substituted with brown sugar.
- Amchoor is a dried mango powder that can be substituted with lemon or lime juice.

FATS AND SHORTENINGS

Lighter oils provide better flavours, and preferences differ regionally. Think coconut oil or mustard oil, which are more pungent and add unique flavour, but do not think you are defying the norm by using your own preference, be it sunflower seed oil, vegetable oil, or peanut oil. Cream is also very important for the preparation of many Indian dishes, especially those coming from the North.

BROWNED ONIONS

Whip up a quantity of browned onion, commonly called for in Indian cooking, and refrigerate it chopped or sliced, ready on hand when needed.

CHAPATI DOUGH

An Indian dish is simply not complete without Indian breads. Whether roti, paratha, chapati, or poori, as a meal accompaniment or choc-a-block with a spread or filling of leftovers, dough can be refrigerated for a up to four days.

Another idea is to make up a batch of the breads to freeze, ready whenever needed. Here is a quick and simple recipe for easy preparation:

Ingredients

- ◆ 3 cups flour
- ◆ 1 tbsp ghee
- ◆ 1 cup warm water
- ◆ 1 ½ tsp salt

Preparation:

1. Combined flour and salt in large bowl and mix in the ghee.
2. Form a dough by pouring in warm water and mixing. Knead the dough for approximately 10 mins. Form into a ball and wrap in plastic. Set aside to rest for an hour.
3. Form dough into six equal sized ball and roll each out to a diameter of approximately 20cm (8-inches) with a chapati rolling pin on a floured surface.
4. Heat a dry griddle/cast iron pan and cook chapatis one at a time for 1 minute each side. When puffed and browned, help form air bubbles by pressing lightly with a spatula around the edges. Serve warm or store in fridge/freezer after cooling,

Equipment

Cooking Vessels

Karai

Consider this the Indian version of a wok, which is a veritable must and versatile addition for preparing Indian cuisine. It is typically copper-bottomed and can be used to cook, deep fry, fry, and sauté. If a copper-bottomed type is not an option, try the heavy bottomed Chinese Wok over a stainless steel variety, which is prone to burn the food.

Pressure Cooker

Comes into its own when cooking the many Indian foods, which require a constant heat over a prolonged period of time, to soften foods such as stewing meats, legumes and pulses. Pulao rice may even be cooked conveniently and quickly in the pressure cooker, making it ideal for so much more than just less than tender cuts of meat, beans and lentils.

Tadka pans

Tadka are the fried spices sprinkled over many Indian dishes to add flavour and authenticity. Spices are quickly fried in exceedingly hot oil, and this small, deep, round pan requires only a little oil and prohibits oil splatters. The long handles distance the exposed flesh from the hot oil.

Tawa

This traditional Indian skillet has as specialised place of importance in cooking flatbreads and roasting spices, or to a lesser extent to fry bread or make crepes.

Idli Cooker

Thick stainless-steel vessel with copper bottom and stainless steel rack in which to add batter for steaming. Trays are stacked in idli cooker with sufficient water to steam while keeping bottom idli dry.

Handi

This deep pot with a wide rim is readily used for cooking foods requiring slow cooking, such as rice, biryani, pilau, and dum.

Degchi

Used similarly to the handi to slow cook Indian food, its hallmark extremely heavy bottom controls heat transferral perfectly, thereby, preventing burning food while guaranteeing even cooking. It is great to boil milk and for making puddings.

Tools and Equipment

The Chakla belan

A very handy pair for the making of flat breads, chapati, naan breads, roti and the like. The Chakla is a round, wooden elevated board on which it is easy to roll out flatbreads and the like. The belan is a small wooden rolling pin, much smaller than the well-known European and American counterparts. As a team they are more than worth their weight in gold and then some in the making of flat breads.

Spice grinders

If you're to cook Indian style, you are going to need spices in a big way. The fresher the better to ensure a flavoursome meal. Which is where the spice grinder becomes essential equipment in any kitchen worth its salt (or quality garam masala, as it were).

Colander

For a style of cooking that requires such plentiful use of vegetables, a colander is essential for cleaning and straining prior to cooking.

Masala dabba

A compact, easy to clean, stainless steel, round spice box which holds 7 main spices in individual pots, and includes the little spoon.

Chimta (chippio)

A sturdy pair of tongs made of stainless steel with pointed tips, perfectly styled to lightly char rotis over a flame, and to flip flatbreads on a tawa.

Jhaara

Perforated round metal spatula ideal to drain oil from foods removed from the karai, or to turn snacks and desserts during frying for even browning.

Charni (sifter)

To ensure a dough with a smooth consistency that is not clumpy when making Indian flatbreads scratch, the flour is sifted through this ultra-fine mesh set in a tall metal rim. Yoghurt can also be strained through it when lined with clean cheesecloth.

Breakfast

Understandably in such a vast country, breakfasts vary regionally. In Northern India paranthas, poori sabji, and poha are more likely to be on offer. Paranthas are pan fried Indian breads stuffed with cooked potatoes, leafy veg, cauliflower, or cheese, served with pickles, curd, or butter. Poori small circular wholewheat breads, deep fried in ghee and served with potato-based curries. Poha is made with rice flattened into dry flakes which swell when hydrated and are eaten with hot or cold liquid, usually water or milk.

South Indian breakfasts almost certanly include Idlis and Dosas. Idli is a savoury rice cake of sorts, favoured as a dish in Indian breakfasts, served hot with Coconut chutney, Sambar and tomato chutney, particualrly in South India. Idlis are made from a fermented batter of rice and black gram lentils, which is steamed in an Idli vessel. Dosas are fermented pancakes made with rice batter and black lentils and served with vegetable stew.

Breakfast Recipes

Vegetable Rava Upma

Time: 35 minutes | Serves: 4

Ingredients:

- 1cup Semolina
- 2.5cm (1 inch) Ginger, grated
- 2 Green Chillies, finely chopped
- 1 finely chopped Onion
- 5 Curry leaves, finely chopped
- Peeled & diced Carrot
- 12 finely chopped Green beans
- 1 tsp Mustard seeds
- 1 tsp halved White Urad Dal (Split)
- ¼ tsp Asafoetida
- Cooking oil
- 3 tbsp Ghee
- Juice of 1 lemon
- ½ tsp Sugar
- Salt

Preparation:

1. Pressure cook carrots and beans with two tbsp water for 1 whistle. Remove from heat and release pressure. Drain water and set aside.

2. Mix 3 cups water, salt and a dash of sugar to a saucepan, bring to boil and set aside.

3. Add mustard seeds and ½ the urad dal seeds to a heavy base pan of heated oil over medium heat. Allow seeds to crackle. Add ginger, onions, curry leaves, asafoetida, and green chilles. Sauté until tender and then add semolina, and sauté until browned with a lightly roasted aroma.

4. Gradually add hot water, stirring continuously. Reduce heat, cover and simmer. Stir regularly for 10 minutes to avoid lumps.

5. Stir in steamed vegetables, ghee, and lemon juice. Sauté over low heat.

6. Serve with Rava Kesari Bhath and Coconut Chutney.

Vegetable Semiya Upma

Time: 45 minutes | Serves: 4

Ingredients:

- 2 cups roasted Semiya
- 1 tsp Mustard seeds
- 1 tsp White Urad Dal
- ½ tsp Asafoetida
- Finely chopped sprig Curry leaves
- ¼ tsp Cinnamon
- ¼ tsp Cardamom
- ½ tsp Turmeric
- Finely chopped Onion
- 2.5cm (1 inch) Ginger, grated
- 1 finely diced Carrot
- 6 finely chopped Green beans
- Red chilli powder, to taste
- 1 Lemon for juice
- 1 tsp Sugar
- Salt
- 2 finely chopped sprigs Coriander leaves

Preparation:

1. Heat 2 tbsp of oil in a heavy-base pan, and heat mustard seeds until they crackle. Add urad dal and roast to a light brown. Add ginger, curry leaves, and onions, and sauté for a min.

2. Add vegetables and sauté for a minute until still crunchy. Add roasted semiya, cinnamon powder, cardamom, turmeric, red chilli powder, sugar and salt.

3. Sprinkle cup of water over vermicelli mixture. Stir. Reduce heat, cover and simmer for 10 mins/until water is almost absorbed. Uncover and stir. Gradually add another ½ cup of water to cook upma, if required. Cover and steam over medium heat until cooked.

4. Remove from heat and keep covered for 5 minutes. Stir in lemon juice, coriander leaves and tbsp of ghee.

5. Stir in steamed vegetables, ghee, and lemon juice. Sauté over low heat until well combined.

6. Serve with Coconut or Tomato Chutney.

Upma Kozhukattai

Time: 50 minutes | Serves: 4

Ingredients:

- 2 cups Rice rava
- ½ cup grated Fresh coconut
- ½ tsp Mustard seeds
- ½ tsp White Urad Dal (Split)
- 2 Green Chillies, finely chopped
- 2.5cm (1 inch) Ginger, finely chopped
- 2 finely chopped sprigs of Curry leaves,
- Salt
- ¼ tsp SSP Asafoetida
- 1 tbsp Sesame Oil

Preparation:

1. Heat oil in pressure cooker, add mustard seeds and urad dal and allow seeds to crackle, roast and lightly brown.

2. Stir in ginger, curry leaves, green chillies, asafoetida and soaked idli rava. Stir fry until lightly roasted, approximately 3 or 4 mins.

3. Stir in 4 cups of water, coconut, and salt and cover. Cook for 3 to 4 whistles. Remove from heat, allow the pressure to release, open, stir and cool slightly.

4. For the Kozhukattai, prepare steamer with steamer plates or idli plates greased with oil. Divide the cooled rice upma mixture into 20 equal portions. Arrange these dumplings on steamer plates and place into steamer. Steam over high heat for 10 minutes. Remove from heat, and remove Upma Kozhukattai from steamer. Set aside before serving.

5. Serve with Puli Inji.

Karnataka Sooji Upma

Time: 35 minutes | Serves: 4

Ingredients:

- 2 cups Sooji
- 2.5cm (1 inch) grated Ginger
- 1 finely chopped Onion
- 2 finely chopped Green Chillies
- 1 cup steamed Peas
- 1 tsp Chana dal
- 1 tsp Mustard seeds
- ½ tsp White Urad Dal (Split)
- ¼ tsp Asafoetida
- 2 tbsp Cooking oil
- 4/5 Curry leaves
- 1 tbsp grated coconut
- Small bunch, finely chopped Coriander leaves
- Salt

Preparation:

1. Dry roast semolina in skillet over medium heat until it releases a roasted aroma and is slightly golden. Set aside.
2. Heat tsp oil in heavy-base pan. Add mustard seeds and allow to crackle, stir in channa dal and urad dal. Roast over medium heat.
3. Stir in ginger, onion, green chillies, and curry leaves and sauté until soft. Add 4 cups of water, peas, and salt and bring to boil. Add sooji, stirring continuously.
4. Stir until thickened, reduce heat, cover, and simmer.
5. Serve hot, garnished with fresh coriander leaves and grated coconut, accompanied by South Indian Coconut Chutney or curds.

Vegetable Oats Upma

Time: 45 minutes | Serves: 4

Ingredients:

- 1 cup Instant rolled Oats
- ¼ cup diced & steamed Carrots
- ¼ cup chopped & steamed Green beans
- ¼ cup steamed Green peas
- ¼ cup finely chopped Onion
- 1 tsp grated Ginger
- 1 chopped Green Chilli
- 5/6 finely chopped Curry leaves
- ¼ cup finely chopped Tomatoes
- ¼ tsp Turmeric powder
- ½ tsp Mustard seeds
- 1 tsp White Urad Dal
- Halved Dry red chilli
- 1 tbsp Cashew nuts, roasted in ghee
- 1 tbsp Cooking oil
- Salt, to taste
- Few, chopped Coriander leaves
- Grated Fresh coconut, for garnish

Preparation:

1. Dry roast rolled oats in a heavy-base pan until lightly crisp with a roasted aroma. Remove, set aside and allow to cool.

2. In the same heavy-base pan, heat oil and add mustard seeds, red chillies, and urad dal, cooking until mustard seeds crackle and chilli & urad dal are roasted to a light brown.

3. Add green chillies, ginger, onion, and curry leaves and sauté until soft. Add turmeric powder, steamed vegetables tomatoes and salt, and sauté for 30 seconds.

4. Add oats, stir well until combined and cover pan. Reduce heat and steam for a few mins.

5. Serve garnished with grated coconut and coriander leaves alongside raw Mango Coconut Chutney Recipe.

Broken Wheat Upma

Time: 30 minutes | Serves: 4

Ingredients:

- 1 cup Broken wheat Rava
- ¼ cup finely chopped Onions
- ¼ cup finely chopped Carrot
- ¼ cup finely chopped Green beans
- ¼ cup small Cauliflower florets
- ½ tsp Cumin seeds
- ½ tsp Mustard seeds
- 6 finely chopped Curry leaves
- 2 tsp chopped Green Chillies
- ¼ tsp Turmeric powder
- ¼ tsp Asafoetida
- 1 tsp grated Ginger
- 1 tsp Ghee
- 1 tsp Oil
- 2 tbsp Coriander leaves, chopped
- Salt

Preparation:

1. Presure cook beans, carrots, and cauliflower with a pinch of salt in 2/3 tbsp water for 1 whistle. Remove from heat and release the pressure immediately.

2. Heat oil in pressure cooker. Cook mustards seeds and cumin until they crackle. Add onions and curry leaves and sauté until onions are tender.

3. Add green chillies, broken wheat, turmeric powder, asafoetida, and salt. Stir over medium heat for 1 min until dalia has a roasted aroma. Add 1½ cups water, cover and cook for 2 - 3 whistles. Remove from heat and allow the pressure to release by itself.

4. Stir cooked veggies into broken Wheat Upma, and adjust salt to taste.

5. For a diabetic friendly breakfast, stir in fresh coriander leaves and serve hot with coconut chutney and sliced bananas.

Vegetable Oats Upma

Time: 45 minutes | Serves: 4

Ingredients:

- 1 cup Instant rolled Oats
- ¼ cup diced Carrots, steamed
- ¼ cup chopped Green beans, steamed
- ¼ cup Peas, steamed
- ¼ cup finely chopped Onion
- 1 chopped Green Chilli
- 1 tsp grated Ginger
- 5 to 6 finely chopped Curry leaves
- ¼ cup finely chopped Tomatoes
- ½ tsp Mustard seeds
- ¼ tsp Turmeric
- 1 tsp White Urad Dal (split)
- 1 tbsp Cashew nuts, roasted in ghee
- 1 halved Dry red chilli
- 1 tbsp Cooking oil
- Salt
- Chopped coriander leaves
- Grated Fresh coconut to garnish

Preparation:

1. Dry roast rolled oats in a heavy-base pan until it becomes lightly crisp with a roasted aroma. Remove, set aside and allow to cool.

2. In the same heavy-base pan, heat oil and add red chillies, mustard seeds, and urad dal, cooking until mustard seeds crackle and red chilli and urad dal are roasted to a light brown.

3. Add onion, green chillies, ginger and curry leaves and sauté until soft, then add turmeric powder, salt, steamed vegetables and tomatoes and sauté for half a minute more.

4. Add oats, stir well until combined. Cover pan, reduce heat and allow to steam for a few minutes.

5. Serve garnished with coriander leaves and freshly grated coconut and raw Mango Coconut Chutney Recipe for a healthy breakfast.

Instant Oats Idli

Time: 15 minutes | Serves: 6-7 Idlis

Ingredients:

- ¾ cup of oats (before powdering)
- ½ cup Sooji/Semolina
- 1 cup Curd
- Just less than ½ tsp baking soda
- Salt
- For the seasoning:
- 2 tsp Oil
- ¾ tsp Cumin seeds
- 1 tsp Mustard seeds
- Pinch of Urad dal
- Pinch of Hing
- ¼ tsp crushed Whole black pepper
- 2.5cm (1 inch) finely chopped Ginger
- Finely chopped Green chilli
- 1 grated Carrot
- Chopped coriander leaves
- Curry leaves

Preparation:

1. Dry roast oats and sooji until slightly hot to touch. Grind oats and set aside.

2. Heat mustard seeds in 2 tsp oil until they crackle. Add remaining seasoning ingredients and cook to delightful fragrance.

3. Mix powdered oats, rava, curd, salt, baking soda, and seasoning into the dropping consistency of idli batter with water. Set aside for 14 - 16 mins.

4. Prepare and grease Idli moulds, and bring water to boil. Ladle batter into the prepared idly mould. Steam for 15 min or until the idlis are cooked. Cool slightly, remove from mould and serve hot with chutney or sambar of your choice.

Instant Oats Rava Idli

Time: 30 minutes | Serves: 4

Ingredients:

- 1-½ cup Instant Oats
- ½ cup Sooji/Semolina
- 1 cup Curd/Yogurt
- 1 grated Carrot
- Bunch Coriander, finely chopped leaves
- ½ tsp Enos fruit salt
- Salt

- Ingredients for seasoning:
- 1 tsp Cooking oil
- ½ tsp Mustard seeds
- Sprig finely chopped curry leaves
- ¼ tsp Asafoetida (hing)
- 2 finely chopped Green Chillies
- 1 tbsp Chana dal
- 1 tbsp broken Cashew nuts

Preparation:

1. Heat mustard seeds in oil over medium heat in a skillet until they splutter, add chana dal and roast to golden brown. Add curry leaves, green chilies, and asafoetida and sauté. Remove from heat and leave to cool.

2. Dry roast oats in separate pan over medium heat until roasted aroma. Allow to cool. Grind to a powder and set one side.

3. Mix oats powder, roasted sooji, roasted seasoning ingredients, coriander leaves, and grated carrots in large bowl until well combined.

4. Add yogurt, and salt, and gradually add water to form thick batter slightly looser than idli batter. Set aside for between 10 and 15 mins during which time batter will thicken. Add Enos fruit salt and mix some more.

5. Preheat idli steamer with water & grease idli plates with oil. Pour batter into the idli plate. Place Oats Rava Idli in steamer and steam for between 10 and 15 mins.

Quick and Easy Bread Upma

Time: 45 minutes | Serves: 4

Ingredients:

- 16 slices of toasted and buttered bread, cut into dices
- 3 chopped Tomatoes
- 2 sliced Onions
- 2 finely chopped Green Chillies
- 1 tsp Sambar Powder
- 1 tsp Turmeric powder (Haldi)
- 1 tsp Mustard seeds
- 3 sprig Curry leaves
- Salt
- Butter for cooking
- 2 sprigs finely chopped Coriander (Dhania) leaves

Preparation:

1. Heat oil in kadai over medium heat and add mustard seeds. Allow to crackle, add onions and green chillies. Sauté onions over medium heat until soft, add tomatoes, turmeric powder, curry leaves, and sambar powder. Stir over heat until tomatoes soften. Add salt and buttered toast dices, stir to combine and stir fry over medium to high heat for two minutes

2. Stir in chopped coriander leaves to serve

Ragi Rava Idli

Time: 45 minutes | Serves: 4

Ingredients:

- 1 cup Ragi Flour
- 1 cup Sooji/Semolina
- 1 cup Curd
- 2 finely chopped Green Chillies
- 2.5cm (1 inch) finely chopped Ginger
- 1 tsp Enos fruit salt, or ½ tsp baking powder
- 1 tsp Cooking oil
- 1 sprig finely chopped Curry leaves
- 1 tsp White Urad Dal
- 1 tsp Mustardseeds
- 1 tsp Oil
- Salt

Preparation:

1. Heat oil in over medium heat, add mustard seeds and urad dal and cook until seeds crackle and brown. Add green chillies, chopped curry leaves, and ginger and remove from heat when spluttering, Remove from heat. Set aside.

2. Combine ragi flour, sooji, yogurt, enos fruit salt, oil and salt in large bowl. Gradually add 1 cup water until thick batter consistency. Rest batter for 15 mins and add water to retain desired consistency if necessary. Season.

3. Stir ragi rava idli batter well to combine. Preheat idli steamer with water and grease idli plates with oil. Pour batter into the idli plate. Steam for 10 mins until test skewer comes out clean. Remove Idli from steamer and set aside for 4 to 6 mins.

4. Sprinkle idlis with water and remove idlis by running a spoon along sides of cavities.

5. Serve with Tomato Chutney and Idli Milagai Podi for a high protein, diabetic South Indian breakfast.

Puffed Rice Upma – Murmura Upma

Time: 30 minutes | Serves: 4

Ingredients:

- 6 cups Puffed rice, prepared as desired
- 1 tbsp Cooking oil
- 1 Ginger, grated
- ½ tsp Mustard seeds
- ½ tsp Cumin seeds
- 10 roughly torn Curry leaves
- ¼ cup Raw Peanuts
- 1 finely chopped Onion
- 2 finely chopped Green Chillies
- ¼ cup steamed Green peas
- 1 roughly chopped Tomato
- 2⅛ tbsp Lemon juice
- ¼ tsp Turmeric powder
- 1 tbsp Coriander Leaves, finely chopped
- Salt

Preparation:

1. Heat a tbsp of oil in kadai over medium heat, add mustard seeds and allow to crackle. Add peanuts and cumin seeds. Roast over medium heat until raw peanuts crisp and have roasted aroma.

2. Add ginger, green chillies, onions, curry leaves and salt. Sauté until transparent and then add peas, tomatoes and turmeric powder. Cook for 5 mins to get tomatoes tender.

3. Stir in prepared Puffed Rice, lemon juice and coriander leaves. Season to taste and serve for a snappy, easy weekday breakfast or a teatime snack.

Ragi Semiya Upma

Time: 50 minutes | Serves: 4

Ingredients:

- 1-½ cups thin Rice Vermicelli Noodles, steamed
- 1 sliced Onion
- 1/3 cup Peas
- 2 Green Chillies
- ½ cup chopped Carrots
- ¼ tsp Asafoetida

- 1 tsp Mustard seeds
- 1 tsp White Urad Dal (Split)
- 1 tsp Ghee
- Sprig Curry leaves
- 1 tsp Lemon juice
- Salt

Preparation:

1. Add ghee to kadai over heat. When warm, add hing and allow to sizzle for half a min. Add urad dal, mustard seeds, and curry leaves, and allow to crackle. Sauté for 1 min/until urad dal is slightly browned.

2. Add onions. Fry until translucent and soft. Add green chillies, parboiled carrots and peas and salt. Cook for 2/3 mins, until veggies are semi cooked.

3. Add steamed ragi vermicelli and toss well until vegetables are combined.

4. Remove from heat. Serve vermicelli with Coconut Chutney, lemon juice, and freshly brewed coffee or tea for a wholesome breakfast.

Vegetable Rice Upma

Time: 60 minutes | Serves: 4

Ingredients:

- 1 cup Rice, soaked for 2hrs in water
- 1 Onion
- 1 Tomato
- 4 chopped Green Chillies,
- 2.5cm (1 inch) grated Ginger
- Sprig Curry leaves
- 1 finely chopped Carrot
- 5 chopped French Green beans

- ¼ cup Green peas
- 2 tbsp Cooking oil
- 1 tsp Mustard seeds
- 2 ½ cups hot water
- 1 tbsp Chana dal
- 1 tbsp White Urad Dal (split)
- Salt
- 1 tbsp Ghee
- Sprig chopped Coriander Leaves

Preparation:

1. Drain water and allow rice to dry on absorbent kitchen towel. Grind rice coarsely to consistency of regular sooji in grinder.

2. Pressure cook chopped carrot, beans, peas and salt in two tbsp water for one whistle. Remove from heat and release pressure. Set vegetables aside.

3. Cook mustard seeds in heated oil over medium heat in a kadai until they crackle. Add urad dal and chana dal and sauté for a minute until golden brown. Add onions, green chillies, ginger pieces and curry leaves, saute until onions are translucent, add tomatoes, and cook to soft and mushy consistency, about 2 min.

4. Add salt and veg and cook for 1 min while stirring.

5. Add 2 ½ cups hot water, when it comes to rolling boil, reduce heat, add freshly ground rice rava. Stir, cover and cook for 3 to 4 mins.

6. Uncover, add dash of ghee and remove from heat.

7. Garnish with finely chopped dhania, serve with Indian Coconut Chutney and Kumbakonam Filter Coffee.

Ragi & Oats Rava Idli

Time: 40 minutes | Serves: 4

Ingredients:

- 1 cup Ragi Flour
- ½ cup Instant Oats
- 1 cup Sooji (Semolina)
- 1 cup Curd/Yogurt
- 2.5cm (1 inch) finely chopped Ginger
- 2 finely chopped Green Chillies
- 2 tsp Enos fruit salt OR 1 tsp baking powder
- 1 tsp Mustard seeds
- 2 tsp Cooking oil
- Sprig finely chopped Curry leaves
- Salt
- Finely chopped Coriander Leaves

Preparation:

1. Combine ragi flour, oats, yogurt, semolina and salt in large mixing bowl. Gradually add 1 cup water to reach thick batter consistency. Set aside for 10 to 15 mins.

2. Add mustard seeds and curry leaves to oil over medium heat in pan and heat until seeds crackle. Remove from heat; set aside.

3. Adjust the batter as required to thick pouring consistency. Add seasoning, ginger, green chillies, enos fruit salt/baking powder and 1 tbsp of oil and stir well.

4. Preheat idli steamer and grease the idli plates. Fill mould cavities with Ragi Oats batter and place in steamer. Steam the idlis for 10 to 15 mins until a skewer comes out clean when inserted in centre.

5. Remove Idli from steamer and set aside for 5 mins. Sprinkle idlis with water and remove idlis by running a spoon along the sides of the cavities.

6. Serve with Peanut Chutney and Idli Milagai Podi.

Veggie Rava Idli

Time: 40 minutes | Serves: 4

Ingredients:

- 1½ cup Sooji (Semolina)
- 1 cup Curd (Yogurt)
- 1 tbsp grated Ginger
- ½ cup Peas
- ½ cup Sweetcorn
- ½ cup grated Carrot
- ½ cup finely chopped Coriander Leaves
- 3 to 4 finely chopped Green Chillies
- 1 tbsp Mustard seeds
- ½ tbsp Chana dal
- 1 tbsp Oil
- 10 Curry leaves
- 1 cup Water
- 1 tsp Enos fruit salt
- Salt

Preparation:

1. Whisk together semolina, yoghurt and water in large bowl. Mix in peas, corn, carrot, ginger, coriander, green chillies, and salt.

2. Add mustard seeds, green chilies chana dal, and curry leaves to heated oil in tadka pan. Sauté over medium heat for 1 minute. Remove from heat.

3. Mix together tadka and yoghurt mixture and enos fruit salt.

4. Preheat idli steamer and grease the idli plates. Ladle Idli batter into moulds, place in steamer and steam for 12 to 15 mins. Remove from mould after 15 mins if skewer comes out clean.

5. Serve for breakfast with Tomato Garlic Chutney.

Lunch Recipes

Chana Kulcha

. . . .

Time: 40 minutes | Serves: 2

A Punjabi delicacy of spiced chickpeas and Indian bread

Ingredients:

- 1kg (2.2lb) Chickpeas
- 2 tsp Baking Soda
- Masala:
- 3 tsp Salt
- 2 tsp Mango Powder
- 1 tsp red Chilli Powder
- 2 tsp Black Pepper

- 2 tsp Cumin
- 2 tsp Cloves, powdered
- 2 tsp dry Ginger
- 2 tsp Coriander
- 2 tsp Carom
- 2 tsp Cinnamon

Preparation:

1. Soak Chickpeas overnight in water/baking soda solution. Bring to boil. Simmer over low heat for 6 to 7 hrs.

2. Add salt, mango powder, red chilli powder, black pepper, cumin, cloves, ginger, coriander, carrom and cinnamon. Mix well. Serve hot with kulchas.

Allahabad ki Tehri

Time:1 hour 24 minutes Serves: 6

Ingredients:

- 100ml (4oz) Mustard oil
- 4 Brown cardamoms
- 8 Green cardamoms
- 2 Bay leaves | 8 Cloves
- 2 Sticks Cinnamon
- 8 to 10 Black peppercorns
- 50g (2oz) chopped Garlic
- 50g (2oz) chopped Ginger
- 3-4 Green chillies, chopped
- 2 Onions, chopped
- 2 tbsp ground Cumin seeds
- 2 tbsp Coriander seeds, ground
- ½ tsp Turmeric | ½ tsp Red chili powder
- ½ tsp Asafoetida, dissolved in water
- 5 Potatoes, boiled & chopped
- 3 chopped Carrots
- 100g (3.5oz) chopped Green Beans
- 100g (3.5oz) chopped Cauliflower
- Salt | 200g (7oz) Curd
- 6 Cups Vegetable stock
- 2 ½ Cups Basmati rice
- 50ml (1.8oz) Ghee | 1 Bunch Coriander | 1 Lime

Preparation:

1. Heat mustard oil in heavy-based pan, and stir in bay leaves, cinnamon sticks, green & brown cardamom, green chilli, cloves, onions, garlic, ginger and peppercorn, heating for 2 maybe 3 mins.

2. Add cumin, red chilli powder, coriander seeds, turmeric, asafoetida and water and cook for 5 to 6 mins. Add potatoes, carrots, beans, cauliflower and salt to taste. Simmer for 14 -16 mins.

3. Stir in curd and mix well. Add basmati rice and stir until evenly coated. Pour in vegetable stock, cover and simmer over low heat.

4. Serve garnished with lime juice, drizzle of ghee, and sprinkle of fresh coriander.

Low Fat Dahi Chicken

Time:1 hour 19 minutes Serves: 4

*This simple common Hyderabadi Indian chicken curry
incorporates yogurt/curd and chicken and may be prepared in various ways*

Ingredients:

- 500g (1.1lb) boneless chicken
- 2 ½ cups Yogurt
- 1 tsp Garlic paste
- 1 tsp Cumin
- ½ tsp red Chilli Powder
- A little less than ¼ tsp Turmeric
- ¼ tsp Garam Masala
- Slit green Chillies
- 2 chopped Onions
- 1 chopped Tomato
- Coriander leaves
- 2 tsp oil
- 1 tsp salt

Preparation:

1. Mix yogurt, cumin, garlic paste, red chilli powder, garam masala, and turmeric with your hands. Add slit chillies and chicken. Set aside for 30 mins.

2. Meanwhile cook onions in pan in 2 tsp oil until translucent and soft. Add tomatoes, cook for 1 min, and then add the chicken. Marinade and cook to desired consistency. Season to taste.

3. Serve garnished with coriander leaves alongside rice and naan or roti.

Kolhapuri Vegetables

Time: 45 minutes | Serves: 4

A mixed vegetable dish in thick, spicy gravy served with chapatis, originating in Kolhapur, Maharashtra, India.

Ingredients:

- 500g (1.1lb) chopped mixed vegetables
- 2 tbsp yogurt mixed with ginger-garlic paste & set aside for 3-4 hrs
- 1 tsp Ginger-garlic Paste
- 2 tsp Lemon juice
- 1 ½ tsp salt
- 2 tbsp Oil
- ½ cup grated Onion
- Dry roast separately and grind:
- ¼ Cinnamon
- ½ tsp Cloves
- ¼ tsp Peppercorns and black Cumin
- ¼ tsp broken up Mace
- ¼ dry grated Coconut
- 1 tbsp Coriander seeds
- 1 tsp Dagar phool
- 2 Kashmiri mirchi

Preparation:

1. Combine vegetables, yogurt, ginger-garlic paste, lemon juice, salt and grated onions and set aside.

2. Stir-fry onions in heated oil until lightish brown. Add ground masala, and sauté. Add vegetable mixture. Bring to boil, reduce heat and simmer for 4 mins. Serve hot.

Black Channa and Coconut Stew

Time: 55 minutes | Serves: 2

Ingredients:

- ½ chopped Medium Onion
- 2.5cm (½ inch) Ginger, minced
- 2 to 3 Garlic cloves
- ½ Lemon Grass stalk
- Lime leaves
- 2 Green chilies, halved lengthwise
- 2 diced Eggplants
- 60g (2oz) diced Zucchini
- 60g (2oz) diced Bottle Gourd

- 90g (3oz) Black Channa, cooked
- 60ml (2oz) bean cooking liquid
- 100ml (3.5oz) Coconut Milk
- 2 tbsp Harissa Paste
- Basil leaves
- Bunch of coriander
- Bunch of parsley
- Salt & Pepper

Red/Yellow Chillies

Preparation:

1. Dice the washed and dried zucchini, gourd and eggplant, and leave in bowl of chilled salted water.

2. Grind ginger, garlic, green chillies, lime leaves, lemon grass & salt to paste.

3. Heat oil in casserole or heavy bottomed dish, and fry onions. Drain diced veg and sweat them with the onions. Add cooked black channa and paste and sauté for 5 mins before mixing in 2 tbsp harissa paste and cooking for 5 mins. Add bean liquid, pepper, salt and ladle in coconut milk. Heat through.

4. Serve garnished with coconut.

Urlai Roast

Time: 30 minutes | Serves: 4

Ingredients:

- Chettinadu masala:
- 1 Coconut, grated
- 10g (0.35oz) Whole red Chillies
- 15g (0.4oz) Coriander seeds
- 15g (4oz) Ginger | 15g (4oz) Garlic
- 1 tsp cinnamon
- 1 tsp cardamoms
- 1 tsp cloves | ½ tsp Kalpasi bark
- ½ tsp Star Anise seeds
- 1 tsp black Pepper Corns
- 3g (1oz) Curry Leaves | ½ tsp Turmeric
- Urlai roast:

- 500g (1lb) Small Potatoes, boiled
- 3 chopped Tomatoes
- 4 chopped Onions
- 1 tsp Chettinadu masala
- 2 tbsp Oil | ½ tsp Ginger garlic Paste
- 3 slit green Chillies
- 5 to 6 Curry leaves
- ¼ tsp Turmeric | 2 tsp red Chilli powder
- 4 tsp Coriander | ½ cup water
- Coriander leaves

Preparation:

1. Roast coriander seeds, coconut, cinnamon, cardamoms, ginger, garlic, whole red chillies, star anise seeds, cloves, kalpasi bark, curry leaves, black peppercorns, turmeric and grind to fine paste. Set aside.

2. Sauté onions until translucent, add ginger garlic paste, tomatoes, green chillies, curry leaves, turmeric, red chillies, coriander and salt.

3. Keep heat constant and add water, chicken, boiled potatoes and chettinadu masala. Cook to reduce for up to 4 mins.

4. Serve hot with appams or rice, garnished with coriander leaves and fresh red or yellow chillies.

Lamb–Fry

Time: 30 minutes | Serves: 4-6

Ingredients:

- 2 cups thinly sliced Onion
- 3 tbsp vegetable Oil
- 1 tsp Garlic
- 1 tsp Ginger
- 1 tsp Green chili (serrano, jalapeño or Thai)
- 3 tsp ground Coriander
- ½ tsp Cumin
- ¼ tsp Cayenne pepper
- ½ tsp Black Pepper
- Pinch Turmeric
- Pinch Cinnamon
- Pinch Ground Cloves
- 2 tbsp Water
- 900g (2 lbs) 2cm (¾-inch) cubed Leg of Lamb
- ½ tsp fresh Lemon juice
- Salt

Preparation:

1. Brown onion in oil over medium-high heat in pan and stir in garlic, ginger, and green chili, cooking for 1 min.

2. Form paste with ground spices and water. Add to onion mixture. Stir until fragrance is released.

3. Add lamb and salt. Fry over medium heat, stirring frequently for 10 to 15 mins. Season to taste, stirring in lemon juice. Remove from heat.

Rava Dosas with Potato Chickpea Masala

Time: 1 hour | Serves: 4

Ingredients:

- For masala filling:
- 680g (1 ½ lbs) baby potatoes
- 1/3 cup dried desiccated unsweetened Coconut
- 2 tsp Cumin seeds
- 1 tbsp Curry powder
- ½ tsp Cinnamon
- ½ tsp Turmeric
- 8cm (3-inch) fresh jalapeño with seeds, coarsely chopped
- Smashed Garlic cloves 6.5cm (2 ½ -inch) Ginger, coarsely chopped
- 3 ⅓ cup vegetable Oil
- 1 ¾ cups water, divided

- 1 can Chickpeas, drained and rinsed
- 1 large chopped Onion
- ½ cup frozen peas (not thawed)
- ½ cup chopped Coriander Leaves
- For rava dosas:
- ½ cup all-purpose Flour
- ½ cup Semolina flour
- ½ cup Rice flour
- ½ tsp Cumin seeds
- 2 cups water
- Pinch Salt
- Vegetable oil for brushing

Preparation:

1. Make Masala filling by cutting peeled potatoes into 4cm (1 ½ -inch) chunks. Cover with cold water and set aside.

2. Toast coconut in heavy skillet over medium heat for 3/4 mins, stirring occasionally until golden. Remove and wipe skillet clean. In skillet, toast cumin seeds for half minute over medium heat, until fragrant. Remove and reserve skillet.

3. Purée jalapeño, ¼ cup water, garlic, ginger, cinnamon, curry powder, turmeric, oil, and 1 tsp salt. Cook smooth purée over medium-high heat in skillet for 1 min, stirring, until thickened. Add onion and cook another 8 mins until onion softens, stirring occasionally.

4. Drain potatoes, add to onion mixture with cumin seeds and coon over medium heat for 10 mins, stirring occasionally.

5. Add chickpeas and remaining 1½ cups water, scraping brown bits. Simmer covered for 16 to 20 mins. Add peas, cover and cook for 3 mins. Remove from heat and stir in toasted coconut and coriander leaves.

6. Make dosas while potatoes cook:

7. To make dosas, whisk together flours, cumin seeds, water and salt.

8. Brush skillet with oil and heat until it shimmers, over medium-high heat. Swirl ½ cup batter in skillet until base is coated. Cook for 2 mins until edges are golden. Turn and cook another minute. Remove and do same until all batter is converted to dosas, stacking and covering loosely with foil to retain heat.

9. Serve filled generously with masala filling.

Butter Chicken

Serves: 4-6

Ingredients:

- Chicken:
- 900g (2 lbs) boneless, skinless Chicken breast, cut in 2.5 (1 inch) chunks
- 1 tbsp Lemon juice
- 1 cup plain Yogurt
- 1 tbsp grated fresh ginger
- 1 tsp red chili powder
- 3 minced Garlic cloves
- 1 tsp Garam masala
- 1 tsp Turmeric
- 1 tbsp Oil
- Sea Salt
- 2 tbsp Butter, melted
- Curry:
- 4 tbsp Butter
- 2 whole Cloves
- 4 green Cardamom pods
- 1 black Cardamom pod
- 5cm (2-inch) Cinnamon stick
- 8 minced Garlic cloves
- 1 tbsp Ginger
- ½ tsp Fenugreek seed
- ½ red Chili, diced
- ¼ cup Tomato paste
- 1 can crushed tomatoes
- 1 tsp red Chili powder
- 3 cups Chicken stock
- 1 tsp Sea Salt
- 1 tbsp pure Maple syrup
- 1 tbsp dried Fenugreek leaves, crushed
- 1 cup heavy Cream
- 1 tbsp Garam masala
- To serve:
- Heavy cream
- Coriander
- Red Chillies, sliced
- Naan/Rice

Preparation:

1. Toss chicken chunks in chili powder and lemon juice and refrigerate for 19 mins.

2. Combine yogurt, turmeric, garlic, ginger, garam masala, oil, and salt. Work yogurt marinade onto chicken. Cover and refrigerate a minimum 12 hrs, preferably overnight.

3. Preheat oven to 201℃ (400°F). Soak 10 to 12 bamboo skewers in cold water for 20 mins

4. Skewer chicken and bake for 12 mins, turning halfway through. Brush the fowl with melted butter. Set aside.

5. Melt butter in heavy-based pot over medium heat and cook cloves, cinnamon stick, and cardamom pods until fragrant (2 to 3 mins). Add ginger, garlic, tomato paste, chillies, and fenugreek seeds. Cook for 2 mins, stirring often. Add chile powder and tomatoes and cook for further 20 mins, stirring frequently.

6. Remove from heat, purée and return to stir in stock and salt and simmer over medium heat for 16 mins until thickened satisfactorily.

7. Remove chicken from the skewers and add to curry with dried fenugreek leaves and maple syrup. Cook covered for 8 mins. Over medium/low heat, stir in garam masala and cream and simmer for 4 to 6 mins.

8. Serve drizzled with cream and coriander, accompanied with naan or rice. Add sliced red chiles if you prefer a spicy dish.

Shrimp Poached in Coconut Milk with Fresh Herbs

| *Serves: 6*

Ingredients:

- 900g (2 lbs) shrimp, washed, shelled & deveined
- 7 tbsp light vegetable Oil
- 2 cups onions, finely chopped
- 2 tsp Garlic
- 1 ½ tbsp Ginger root, crushed
- Green chilies, seeded & minced
- ¼ tsp Turmeric
- 2 tbsp Coriander
- 3 cups Coconut Milk
- Salt
- 2 tbsp Coriander leaves

Preparation:

1. Heat oil in a heavy-bottomed pan, and fry onions over high heat until golden brown (10 mins) stirring all the time. Reduce to medium heat, add garlic, ginger, and chilies, and fry for a further 2 mins. Add turmeric and coriander and stir rapidly for 15 seconds before addding coconut milk and salt. Cook uncovered until thickened, 10 mins, stirring frequently.

2. Add shrimp. Reduce heat to medium-low, cover and simmer for 5 to 8 mins.

Cumin–Scented Potatoes and Tomatoes

| *Serves: 6*

Ingredients:

- 680g (1 ½ lbs) peeled baby potatoes cut into 10mm (½ -inch) cubes, covered with cold water
- 1 small red Onion, cut into 1cm (½ -inch) cubes
- 2 tbsp Canola Oil
- 1 tbsp Cumin seeds
- 1 tsp Turmeric
- 1 tsp Cayenne pepper
- 2 tsp coarse Salt
- Tomato, cut into 20 mm (1-inch) cubes
- 2 tbsp Coriander leaves & tender stems, finely chopped

Preparation:

1. Drain and pat dry the potatoes.
2. Heat oil in saucepan over medium-high heat and cook cumin seeds until they sizzle (5 to 10 seconds). Add onion, potatoes, and turmeric. Stir-fry for 4 to 6 mins.
3. Add 1 cup water, salt, and cayenne and bring to boil. Reduce heat to medium-low, cover and cook for 19 to 20 mins stirring occasionall. Stir in coriander and tomato. Cover and simmer for 1 to 2 mins, stirring occasionally.
4. Serve with accompaniments.

Chicken Tikka Masala

Time: 45 minutes | Serves: 4

Ingredients:

- For the chicken:
- 680g (1 ½ lbs) skinless, boneless, chicken breasts
- ¼ cup Greek yogurt
- 2 tbsp Peanut Oil
- 2 tsp lime/lemon juice
- 1 large clove garlic, minced
- Sauce:
- 1 ½ tsp Cumin
- ½ tsp Cardamom
- ½ tsp Nutmeg
- 1 ½ tsp Paprika
- ½ tsp Cayenne
- 1 tbsp Coriander
- 1 tbsp Ginger, grated
- 4 tbsp unsalted Butter
- 1 white onion, finely chopped
- 1 ½ cups canned tomato purée
- ¾ cup water
- ½ cup heavy cream
- 1 ¼ tsp Salt
- ½ tsp Black pepper
- ½ cup chopped fresh Coriander and sprigs to garnish
- For serving:
- Naan
- Cooked Basmati Rice

Preparation:

1. To marinate chicken, prick all over with fork on both sides. Arrange chicken breasts, well spaced, on plastic wrap, covered with another sheet of plastic wrap. Beat to 1.5 to 2cm (½ - to ¾-inch) thickness.

2. Whisk yogurt, 1 tbsp peanut oil, lime juice, and garlic together in small bowl. Add chicken, rubbing marinade over well. Set aside.

3. To make sauce, whisk together coriander, cardamom, grated ginger, nutmeg, cumin, paprika, and cayenne. Melt butter over moderate heat. Add onion and sauté for 5 mins, stirring occasionally, until caramelised. Reduce heat slightly and stir in spice and ginger mixture. Add water, tomato purée, heavy cream, and salt, and bring to boil. Reduce heat and simmer uncovered for 10 minutes.

4. Meanwhile over moderately high heat, add ½ tbsp peanut oil to heavy skillet. Separate chicken into 2 batches and cook, turning often for 6 to 9 mins until both batches are browned and coooked.

5. Slice cooked chicken into 4 cm (1 ½ -inch) pieces. Add to heat and simmer for 5 minutes, stirring occasionally. Remove from heat, stir in chopped coriander, salt, and pepper.

6. Serve garnished with coriander sprigs with naan, and/or Basmati Rice.

Tadka Dhal

Time: 1 hour | Serves: 4

Ingredients:

- 1 ½ cups lentils, well rinsed
- 1 tsp Turmeric
- 2 black Cardamom pods
- 3 tbsp Oil
- 2 tsp Mustard seeds
- 2 Cinnamon sticks
- 1 tsp Cumin seeds
- 6 Cloves
- 4 green Cardamom pods
- 2 finely sliced Scallions,

- 1 tbsp finely chopped Ginger
- 3 - 4 chillies, some chopped, some whole
- 2 cloves garlic, finely chopped
- 6 cherry tomatoes, halved
- Pinch Salt
- 1 tsp Sugar
- Juice of ½ Lemon
- Chopped Coriander

Preparation:

1. Boil lentils in 4 cups far from warm water, stirring in black cardamom pods and turmeric for smoky flavor. Cook for 45 mins/until softened , skimming off foam regularly.

2. To prepare tadka, cook cinnamon sticks, green cardamom pods and cloves in heated oil. Once cardamoms have cooked white, stir in cumin and mustard seeds. When seeds are sizzling, add scallions, garlic, ginger and chillies and cook for a minute.

3. Stir through tomatoes and remove from heat. Float tadka on the dhal. Season with lemon juice, salt and sugar.

Tandoori Chicken

| Serves: 6

Ingredients:

- 3 x 1 to 1.2kg (2 - 2 ¼ lbs) chickens
- 2 ½ tsp Meat tenderiser
- 1/3 cup Lemon juice
- For marinade
- 2 large Garlic cloves
- 1 tsp ground roasted Cumin seeds
- 1 tbsp chopped Ginger root
- ½ tsp ground Cardamom
- ½ tsp red Pepper
- 1 tbsp Paprika
- 1/3 cup plain Yogurt
- Ghee for basting

Preparation:

1. Remove wings and neckbone and quarter chickens. Prick chicken and slash diagonally, 2cm (½ -inch) deep.

2. Rub meat tenderiser and lemon juice all over chicken and into the slashes. Cover and marinate for 29 mins.

3. Blend marinade ingredients until reduced to smooth sauce.

4. Coat the chicken pieces well in marinade, cover and marinate for 4 hours at room temperature, or overnight in refrigerater, turning a few times.

5. If refrigerated, bring chicken to room temperature before cooking.

6. Preheat oven to 270℃ (520°F). Remove chickens from marinade, brush with ghee, roast in extra-large shallow roasting pan for 25 to 30 mins/ until cooked through

7. Brush with ghee. Serve immediately.

Dinner Recipes

Punjabi Lemon Chicken

Time: 1 hour 20 minutes | Serves: 4

Ingredients:

- 6 Skinless Chicken thighs
- For the base:
- 3 to 4 tbsp refined Oil
- 2 tsp Cumin seeds
- 2 Onions, julienne
- 6 chopped Garlic cloves
- 2.5cm (½ inch) chopped Ginger
- 3 to 4 Green Chillies
- ¾ tsp Turmeric
- Salt
- 1 tsp ground Coriander
- 1 cup fresh Lemon juice
- ½ cup Orange juice
- ¼ tsp fresh sugarcane juice
- Fresh coriander

Preparation:

1. Swirl oil to cover heavy cooking vessel and heat over high heat. Saute cumin seeds until crackling and fragrant. Add garlic, onions, and ginger and sauté to golden brown. Up the heat and add spice powders, toasting until aromatic and well toasted. Add water and bhuno the base ingredientsuntil oil rises to the top.

2. Add salt and chicken thighs and increase heat to fry chicken in the masala until evenly coated.

3. Add orange and lemon juice and deglaze the pan, scraping deposits well from base of pan. Stir well, add sugarcane juice to balance the acidity.

4. Bring to boil, reduce heat, cover and simmer over low heat until chicken is just about falling from bone.

5. Uncover and simmer until slightly reduced and remove from heat. Serve with hot rotis or rice and garnished with fresh coriander.

Chettinad Fish Fry

Time: 50 minutes | Serves: 4

Ingredients:

- 2 King fish (Surmai) fillets, in equal portions
- 2 tbsp Oil
- Marinade:
- 7 to 8 Garlic cloves
- 2 tsp Black Peppercorns
- 1 mashed Ginger knob
- 1 tsp Cumin
- 1 tsp Fennel
- 2 tsp Coriander seeds
- ½ tsp Mustard seeds

- 9 to 10 Curry leaves
- Salt
- 1 tsp Oil
- 1 tbsp Water
- ½ chopped tomato
- 2 tsp Turmeric
- 1 tsp red Chilli powder
- 5 tsp Tamarind extract
- Lemon wedges
- 1 tbsp Cornflour for sprinkling

Preparation:

1. Dry roast garlic, curry leaves, ginger, cumin, fennel, coriander seeds, mustard seeds and black peppercorns. Pound to paste and add salt, oil and water as needed.

2. Add turmeric, red chili powder, chopped tomato, salt and tamarind extract. Pound into a pulp and spread over fish pieces. Sprinkle fish with cornflour.

3. Marinade the fish and refrigerate for 15 to 19 mins.

4. Pan fry fish in refined oil.

5. Serve hot with fresh lemon.

Dum Aloo Lakhnavi

Time: 55 minutes | Serves: 4

Ingredients:

- 500g (1lb) Potatoes
- 100g (0.2 lb) Potatoes, mashed
- 100g (0.2 lb) Crumbled Paneer
- 1 tbsp Cream
- 1 tbsp Butter
- 1 tsp red Chilli powder and salt
- 1 tsp Garam masala
- 1 ½ tsp Kasoori methi
- 3 tbsp Ghee

- Onion gravy
- 200g (0.4 lb) Onions
- ½ tsp Garam masala
- 1 tsp Ghee
- Salt
- Tomato gravy
- 200g (7oz) Fresh Tomato puree
- Salt
- 1 tsp Ghee

Preparation:

1. To prepare onion gravy, heat ghee and sauté all ingredients until onions are glossy. Set aside.

2. Prepare tomato gravy by heating ghee and cooking all ingredients for 2 mins. Set aside.

3. Meanwhile deep fry potatoes. Set aside to cool.

4. To make filling, combine paneer and mashed potatoes. Stuff fried potatoes with filling and set aside.

5. Cook onion and tomato gravies in oil until the oil separates. Mix in chilli powder, garam masala, and kasoori methi, and cook for a minute. Stir in butter and cream and mix well, add potatoes and simmer for 3 to 5 mins.

6. Serve and enjoy.

Keema Biryani

Time:1 hour 39 minutes | Serves 4

Ingredients:

- 500g (1 lb) Rice, washed, soaked
- 5-6 raisins, chopped
- 1 cup Almonds, blanched, peeled & cut
- 1 cup Yogurt
- 2 tbsp desi Ghee
- 1 cup sliced Onions
- 1 tbsp Garlic paste
- ½ tsp Ginger paste
- 2 tsp Coriander
- 1 tsp red Chilli powder
- 500g (1 lb) Lamb keema
- 50g (2oz) Butter
- 1 cup Milk
- 1 tbsp Rose Water
- 5 to 6 Mint Leaves
- 1-piece Ginger, sliced
- Garam Masala
- 2 tsp Coriander seeds
- 2 tsp Cumin seeds
- ¾ Cinnamon sticks
- 3 to 4 pods green Cardamom
- black Cardamom
- 5/6 Cloves
- 2 tsp Mace
- Water
- 1 tsp black Peppercorns
- Salt

Preparation:

1. Dry roast cumin seeds, green cardamom, coriander seeds, cinnamon, mace, black peppercorns and cloves. Cool. Grind to powder.

2. Cook sliced onions in heated ghee over low heat.

3. Whisk together yogurt, black cardamom, ginger paste, garlic paste, coriander, and red chilli powder, and mix with onions. Cook for 2 or 3 mins. Mix in the lamb keema and sauté, add garam masala and salt. Cook until done.

4. Add cup water and simmer. In another pan, add keema, butter, milk, almonds and raisins.

5. Boil rice, add rose water and salt, Stir. Place half the rice into jhol, add ginger and mint leaves. Top off with remaining rice. Cook covered.

6. Serve hot.

Dum Paneer Kali Mirch

Time: 55 minutes | Serves: 4

Ingredients:

- 1 tsp Oil
- 2.5cm (1 inch) Cinnamon stick
- 4 Cloves
- 4 Green cardamoms
- 1 fried Onion, browned and blended to paste with water
- 3 tbsp Yogurt
- Paste of 1 tsp ginger, 1 tsp garlic, 4 green chillies
- 1 tsp ground Coriander
- Pepper
- ¾ tsp Cumin
- 1 tsp Salt
- 2 tbsp Cream
- ¼ tsp Paprika
- ¼ tsp Turmeric
- ¼ tsp Garam masala
- 250g (0.55lbs) Paneer
- Coriander & Fresh Mint leaves

Preparation:

1. Heat cloves, cardamoms and cinnamon in oil until fragrant and mix in onion. Cook. Add green chilli paste, ginger, and garlic and sauté. Add yogurt, cook some more before adding coriander, cumin, pepper powder, haldi and red chilli.

2. Add salt, cottage cheese cubes, cream and ½ cup water. Seal pan and cover with lid. Reduce heat and simmer for 14 – 17 mins.

3. Cook uncovered to desired consistency Season to taste.

Shahi Egg Curry

Time: 35 minutes | Serves: 4

Ingredients:

- 4 Eggs, boiled
- 1 tsp chopped Garlic cloves
- 1 chopped Onion
- 2 sliced Green chillies
- 1 tsp chopped Ginger
- 1 tbsp Fresh Cream
- 1 tbsp Curd
- 1 tsp Kasoori methi
- 1 tbsp Chaat masala
- ½ tsp Garam masala
- ½ tsp Red Chilli powder
- 1 tbsp Coriander leaves
- 1 tsp Salt
- 1 tbsp Oil

Preparation:

1. Grind onion, green chillies, garlic and ginger into coarse paste. Sauté in oil until oil is absorbed.

2. Gently shallow roast coriander seeds, ginger, garlic, coconut, whole red chillies, cinnamon, cardamoms, star anise seeds, black pepper corns, curry leaves cloves, kalpasi bark, and turmeric.

3. Whisk together curd and cream in a pan. Add 1 cup water, kasoori methi, garam masala, red chilli powder, and salt. Bring to boil and simmer for 11 mins.

4. Slit boiled eggs and add to pan. Cook for 5 to 7 mins and mix in chaat masala.

5. Heat oil and sauté onions in a pan until translucent

6. Serve garnished with a tsp of cream and coriander leaves.

Malabari Prawn Curry

Time: 55 minutes | Serves: 4

Ingredients:

- To marinade the prawns:
- 12 to 15 Prawns, shelled and deveined
- 1 tbsp Coconut oil
- ¾ tsp Turmeric
- 1 tsp Red Chilli powder
- Salt
- For the spice paste:
- ½ cup desiccated Coconut
- ½ tsp Fenugreek seeds
- 1 tsp Coriander seeds
- To sear the prawns:
- 1 tsp oil
- For the base:
- 1 tsp Coconut oil
- 5 to 6 Shallots
- 4/5 thin Ginger slices
- 2 red Chillies, split
- 3 to 4 Garlic cloves, thinly sliced
- 1 tsp Chilli powder
- 1 tsp Mustard seeds
- ¾ tsp Turmeric
- 2 green Chillies, partly split
- 1 cup Coconut milk
- Salt
- Diced Tomato,
- 1 ½ tbsp Tamarind extract

- Small piece Jaggery
- 7/8 Curry leaves
- ½ cup Peas
- For garnishing:
- 1 tsp Oil
- ½ tsp Mustard seeds
- 4/5 Curry leaves
- 1 tbsp grated Coconut
- 2 Prawns incl. tails

Preparation:

1. To marinate prawns, add prawns to a bowl with turmeric, coconut oil, red chilli powder, and salt. Set aside for 10 mins.

2. To prepare spice paste, dry roast coconut, fenugreek seeds and coriander seeds in a pan. Make fine paste and set aside.

3. Add prawns to 1 tsp oil in heated pan and sear lightly. Retain juices and set aside.

4. Add shallots to coconut oil heated in karai, along with ginger and garlic slices, red and green chillies, and mustard seeds. Allow to splutter.

5. Add turmeric, chilli powder and spice paste and loosen slightly with 2 tbsp coconut milk. Add remaining coconut milk, salt, and curry leaves, stir and add diced tomatoes, tamarind extract, jaggery and peas. Simmer over low heat for 4 to 6 mins.

6. Add seared prawns and simmer for 3 to 4 mins.

7. Heat oil in pan and add mustard seeds, grated coconut and curry leaves. Cook the prawns with tails for 2 mins per side.

8. Serve immediately with fluffy rice.

Makhmali Kofte

Time: 55 minutes | Serves: 4

Ingredients:

- For the koftas:
- ½ Cup (100 g) firmly packed Khoya
- 6 tbsp Maida
- 1/8 tsp Baking Soda
- Ghee for deep-frying
- For the gravy:
- ¼ cup (60 g) Ghee
- ¼ desiccated coconut
- 1 tbsp Ginger, finely chopped

- 2 tbsp Poppy seeds
- 1 tsp Cumin seeds
- 1 tbsp Coriander powder
- 1 tsp Garam masala
- 2 tbsp Cornflour dissolved in ½ cup milk
- Salt & Black pepper
- 2 tbsp Chopped Coriander leaves

Preparation:

1. Prepare koftas by mashing khoya until smooth, add maida and soda. Knead to a firm/pliable dough. Shape into smooth marble sized balls.
2. Heat ghee in a kadahi, reduce heat and fry cube of bread to light brown in lower temperature.
3. Remove bread and add balls taking care to keep them apart. Fry until golden brown over low heat. Remove. Drain. Increase heat momentarily before adding more balls setting cooked koftas aside.
4. Lift out of fat. Drain. Increase heat and then lower again before adding another batch.
5. To prepare gravy, soak cumin and coconut in water for 1 hour. Grind to paste.
6. Heat ghee and cook cumin seeds until they splutter. Add ginger and sauté until light brown.
7. Add coconut paste, garam masala, coriander, salt, and black pepper. Sauté until fat separates. Bring back to boil after adding 3 cups water. Reduce heat and simmer for 6 mins.
8. Add cornflour solution, simmer for 2 mins, add the koftas and simmer for a further 2 to 3 mins.
9. Garnish with cream and the coriander leaves to serve.

Dal Makhani

Time: 50 minutes | Serves: 4

Ingredients:

- 2 cups Sabut urad dal
- 8 cups Water
- Salt
- 2 tsp Shahi jeera
- 1 tbsp sliced Ginger
- 2 cups Tomato puree
- 2 tbsp Butter
- 1 tbsp Oil
- 1 tsp Kasoori methi
- 1 tsp Chilli powder
- 1 tsp Sugar
- ½ cup Cream
- Green chillies, cut lengthwise

Preparation:

1. Add water to dal, 1 tbsp salt and ginger and cook until dal is tender.

2. Heat butter and oil in heavy base pan, add kasoori methi and shahi jeera and when they splutter, add tomato puree, chilli powder, sugar and remaining salt.

3. Stir-fry over high heat till oil separates. Add cooked dal and bring to boil, ensuring the consistency allows dal to move without inhibition when stirred by adding a little water.

4. Uncover. Simmer until blended.

5. Stir-in cream, heat through, garnish with green chillies and serve immediately.

Mutton Do Pyaaza

Time: 60 minutes | Serves: 4

Ingredients:

- 500g (1lb) Mutton portions
- ¼ cup Ghee
- 1 tbsp Cumin seeds
- ½ tsp Fenugreek seeds, roasted & powdered
- 1 tsp Fennel seeds roasted & powdered
- 1 Bay leaf
- 4 Cloves
- 1 tsp Ginger paste
- 1 cup grated Onions
- 1 tsp Garlic paste
- ½ cup Yogurt
- 2 Green chillies, slit
- 2 cups sliced Onions
- 1 tsp Garam masala
- 1 tbsp Coriander powder
- 1 tsp Chilli powder
- 2 tbsp Coriander leaves, chopped
- Whole peppercorns
- ½ tsp Turmeric
- Salt

Preparation:

1. Heat ghee in heavy-based saucepan, add cumin seeds, fennel seeds, cloves, bay leaf, powdered fenugreek, and peppercorns. Allow to splutter before adding garlic and ginger paste and onions. Sauté on high until soft.

2. Add mutton and stir fry over high heat until opaque. Reduce heat and cover. Cook until tender. Add yogurt, stirring to blend over heat without curdling.

3. Cook until fat separates. Add garam masala, chilli powder, turmeric, coriander, green chillies, sliced onions and salt. Cook further over medium heat until fat again separates.

Shrimp Tikka Masala

Time: 45 minutes | Serves: 4

Ingredients:

- 2 tbsp Extra-virgin Olive oil
- 1 thinly sliced large onion
- 3 tbsp grated, peeled Ginger
- 1 tbsp Garlic, finely grated
- 2 tsp Tomato paste
- 2 tsp Garam masala

- 1 cup water
- ½ tsp Chili powder
- 20 (500g) large shrimp with tails (1 lb), deveined, peeled.
- ¼ cup plain Yogurt
- Seasoning

Preparation:

1. Heat oil over medium heat and cook onion until golden (20 mins). Add garlic, ginger, tomato paste, chili powder, and garam masala, and cook for 4 mins until fragrant.

2. Add water and shrimp and cook for about 4 mins. Remove from heat. Stir in yogurt. Season to taste.

Quick Chicken Curry

Time: 60 minutes | Serves: 4

Ingredients:

- 1 kg (2 lbs) skinless, boneless chicken thighs, cut in 8cm (1 ½ -inch) chunks
- 3 tbsp unsalted Butter
- 3 Shallots, halved and thinly sliced
- 2 tbsp Ginger
- 1 cinnamon stick, halved
- ½ tsp Turmeric
- 1 ½ tsp round Coriander
- 2tbsp red finger chilly thinly sliced

- 2 tsp fresh Lemon juice
- 1 400ml can (13.5 ounces) Coconut Milk
- 1 tbsp Sugar
- 1 cup frozen Peas
- 2 cups packed baby Spinach
- Steamed basmati rice
- Salt and freshly ground pepper
- Almonds, and cilantro leaves

Preparation:

1. Season chicken.

2. Melt butter over medium-high heat. Divide chicken into 2 batches and brown for 8 mins per batch, until golden. Set aside.

3. Reduce to low heat, add cinnamon stick and shallots, stir often while cooking until shallots are soft, 8 mins. Add chilli, ginger, and spices, and cook for further half minute, stirring. Add sugar and lemon juice and cook another half minute. Stir in ¼ cup water, coconut milk, chicken, and retained juices. Season and bring just to boil and reduce heat. Simmer for 8 to 10 mins partially covered. Remove from heat. Add peas and spinach & heat through.

4. To serve, top with almonds and cilantro, accompanied with rice.

Lamb Curry

Time: 55 minutes | Serves: 8

Ingredients:

- 3 tbsp Oil
- 2 finely chopped onions
- 3 tbsp peeled & grated Ginger
- 6 cloves Garlic
- Coarse salt
- 75mm (3-inch) Cinnamon stick
- 1 ½ tsp Coriander seeds, crushed
- 2 ¼ tsp Cumin seeds
- ¾ tsp Turmeric
- 2 Cardamom pods
- 2 tsp Tomato paste
- 1.15kg (2 ½) Lamb shoulder, cut to 25mm(1-inch) pieces
- 350g (12 oz) baby potatoes, cut to 25mm (1-inch)
- 2 cups Chicken broth
- 1 bunch Spinach, trimmed and washed

Cilantro, yogurt, Indian pickle/chutney, and flatbread

Preparation:

1. Heat oil over medium-high heat in pressure cooker and cook ginger, garlic, onions, and 1 tsp salt, until onions are translucent, stirring occasionally (3 mins). Add cinnamon stick, coriander, cumin, turmeric, and cardamom. Stir over heat for 30 seconds until spices are fragrant. Add tomato paste and cook for 16 seconds while stirring.

2. Add lamb, potatoes, broth and salt and pressure-cook over high heat to high pressure. Cook for 24 minutes over medium heat. Remove from heat and vent pressure. Add spinach and season.

3. Serve with yogurt, cilantro, Indian chutney and flatbread.

Chicken—and—Squash Curry

Time: 2 hours | Serves: 8

Ingredients:

- 2 large coarsely chopped onions
- 8/10 coarsely chopped cloves garlic
- ½ cup peeled & coarsely chopped Ginger
- ¼ cup + 1 tbsp Oil
- ¼ tsp Cayenne pepper
- 1 whole clove
- 1 tbsp Cumin seeds
- 2 tsp Mustard seeds
- ½ tsp ground Coriander
- ¼ tsp Turmeric

- 2 tbsp Tomato paste
- 4 cups Chicken broth
- 3 Curry leaves or 2 dried Bay leaves
- 1.4kg (3 lbs) bone-in skinned chicken thighs
- 570g (1 ¼ lbs) 25mm (1-inch) Butternut pieces
- Coarse salt
- Cooked basmati rice, yogurt, and cilantro

Preparation:

1. Puree onions, garlic and ginger until smooth.

2. Heat ¼ cup oil, cumin and mustard seeds over medium-high heat in heavy-base pot for 30 to 60 seconds, stirring until fragrant. Add onion mixture.

3. Cook for 8 mins, stirring occasionally. Reduce heat. Cook for 3 mins, stirring frequently until liquid reduces. Add remaining oil and spices and cook for 17 seconds. Add tomato paste and cook for a further 17 seconds while stirring.

4. Add broth, scraping bottom of pot. Add curry leaves. Bring to boil, reduce heat and simmer for 28 mins.

5. Add seasoned chicken and squash to pot, submerging in liquid. Once its boiling, reduce heat. Simmer for 42 mins. Season to taste.

Curried Shrimp and Cauliflower

Time: 25 minutes | Serves: 4

Ingredients:

- 2 tbsp Oil
- Sliced yellow Onion
- 4 cups Cauliflower florets
- 2 cloves Garlic
- 2 tsp Curry powder
- 1 tbsp minced Ginger
- ¾ cups Chicken broth
- 500g (1 lb) large shrimp, peeled and deveined
- Coarse salt
- White rice

Preparation:

1. Heat oil over medium-high heat. Sauté onion, ginger, and garlic, for 4 mins, add curry powder & ½ tsp salt, and sauté for half a minute.

2. Stir in stock and cauliflower, boil, cover and cook for 6 mins. Add shrimp and cook covered for 2 to 4 min, until opaque.

3. Season to taste. Serve over rice.

Snacks and Desserts

Indian sweets are not like western desserts at all. These exotic and aromatic delicacies come in hundreds of varieties made in all the different states in India. In fact, many of the sweets are synonymous with certain states or regions in India. Ingredients common to all Indian sweets are milk, rice, coconut, besan/chickpea flour and semolina. Flavourants include rose water, saffron, and cardamom. Some of these sweets are synonymous with a particular state or place in India.

Snack and Dessert Recipes

Gulab Jamun

Time: 40 minutes

Known as Indian donuts, these delights are rolled by hand into small balls which are then deep fried in oil and dipped into cardamom-laced sugar syrup

Ingredients:

- 300g (10.5oz) Khoya
- 3 tbsp Flour
- 3 tbsp Sugar
- 500ml (0.11oz) Water
- Pinch Saffron
- 200g (10oz) refined Oil

Preparation:

1. Combine khoya and flour, mix together well and form into a ball.
2. For sugar syrup, combine 3 tbsp sugar and 500ml water, adding a little saffron. Deep fry the gulab jamun and add to the sugar syrup.
3. Serve hot.

Gajar Halwa Sunehri Style

Time: 40 minutes

Ingredients:

- 1.5kg (3.3lbs) Carrots, grated
- 10 whole grcen Cardamom
- 2 Cinnamon sticks
- 500g (18oz) Sugar
- 250g (9oz) Ghee
- 400g (14oz) can of Condensed Milk
- 4 pieces gold Vark
- 50g (2oz) Almonds
- 50g (2oz) Pistachios

Preparation:

1. Stir-fry grated carrots continuously until dehydrated. Add cinnamon, green cardamom, and sugar and cook. Add ghee, cook for 5 to 8 mins. Add condensed milk.

2. Decorate with gold vark and serve garnished with almonds and pistachios.

Modak

Time: 40 minutes

These sweet flour dumplings stuffed with coconut, jaggery, nutmeg and saffron are Lord Ganesha, 'Modakpriya', the one who likes modak's favourite sweet. 21 pieces of modak are served as the offering after the puja during ganesh chaturthi.

Ingredients:

- ◆ For the filling:
- ◆ 1 Cup Coconut, grated
- ◆ 1 Cup Jaggery
- ◆ Pinch of Nutmeg
- ◆ Pinch of Saffron

- ◆ For the shell:
- ◆ 1 Cup Water
- ◆ 2 tsp Ghee
- ◆ 1 Cup Rice flour

Preparation:

1. To prepare filling, add grated coconut and jaggery to a heated pan and stir for 5 mins. Add nutmeg and saffron, mix well and cook for 6 mins. Set aside.

2. To prepare modak, boil water and ghee, add salt and flour. And mix well. Cover and cook halfway through. Spread ghee on base of steel bowl in which to properly knead the hot dough. Roll a little dough into a ball, flatten and shape edges into flower pattern.

3. Fill and seal each dough ball. Place balls in muslin cloth and steam for 10 to 15 mins.

Paneer Haryali

Time: 1 hour 11 minutes

Ingredients:

- 500g (1,1lb) Paneer, cubed
- Grind to a paste:
- ¾ cup Coriander leaves
- 2/3 green Chillies
- 2 tsp Ginger
- 8 Black Peppercorns
- 8 Cloves
- ¼ tsp Cinnamon
- 2 black Cardamom, shelled
- 1 tbsp Salt
- ¼ cup Lemon juice
- Desiccated coconut for garnishing

Preparation:

1. Mix lemon juice with ground ingredients. Use this masala paste to marinate the paneer for half an hour.

2. Grill the paneer in a griller or pan-fry in very little oil.

3. Serve hot, garnished with coconut.

Kakori Kebab

Time: 55 minutes

Ingredients:

- 2 cups ground mutton/lamb
- 2 tsp Salt
- 1 tsp Ginger-garlic paste
- Pinch of Black pepper
- Green chillies, chopped
- 2 tbsp chopped Coriander
- 2 tbsp chopped raw Papaya
- 4 Cloves
- 1 Black Cardamom seeds
- 1 tsp Cumin seeds
- 1 Black Mace
- 1/8 tsp Cinnamon
- ¼ tsp Nutmeg
- 2 cups sliced onions (crisped in ½ cup ghee)
- 1 Egg
- ¼ cup bhuna chana, powdered
- Ghee

Preparation:

1. Preheat oven to 220°C (425°F).

2. Mix all ingredients except ghee and set aside to marinate for 4 hrs before grinding to a thick smooth paste. Knead well and mix in the egg and roasted gram. Cover and refrigerate for an hour.

3. Skewer the meat, Place over a drip tray in pre-heated oven and cook for 15-20 mins. Brush with ghee. Cook for 3 mins.

Vegan and Vegetarian

In a nation rich with heritage, religion and culture, vegatarians and vegans are abundant throughout India. India has more vegetarians than the rest of the world put together. In fact, figures indicate that 31% of Indians are vegetarian. In Indian communities, vegetarianism is highest among the Brahmins, Lingayat, and Jain and Vaishnav. Among Muslims the prevalence is significantly lower. Hindus regard cattle as sacred but they do eat meat other than beef. As a nation, the use of vegtables, pulses, nuts and grains is versatile.

Vegan and Vegetarian Recipes

Indian Aloo Gobi

Time: 45 minutes | Serves: 4

Ingredients:

- 3 Potatoes, chopped, boiled and drained
- 1 Cauliflower, chopped
- ½ Onion, sliced
- 1 tsp Coriander
- 1 tsp Cumin
- ½ tsp Turmeric
- ¼ tsp ground Cloves
- ¼ tsp Ginger
- 2 Bay leaves
- 3 tbsp Olive oil
- 1 tbsp Lemon juice
- 1/3 cup water

Preparation:

1. Cook spices in olive oil for 30 seconds. Add onion, potatoes and cauliflower. Cook for further 3 to 5 mins, add lemon juice and water, cover and cook until cauliflower is done, 6 to 8 mins.

Homemade Vegan Naan

Time: 1 hour 15 minutes | Resting time: 90 minutes | Serves: 8

Ingredients:

- 1 tsp Active Dry Yeast
- ½ cup warm Water
- 3 tbsp Soymilk
- 1 tbsp Sugar
- ½ tsp Onion powder
- ½ tsp Garlic powder
- 1 ¾ to 2 cups Bread flour
- 1 tbsp/more Olive Oil

Preparation:

1. Dissolve yeast in warm water and set one side for 11 mins, until it becomes frothy. Stir in the soy milk.

2. Whisk together sugar, 1 ¾ cups flour, garlic powder, onion powder, and salt.

3. Stir together dry and wet ingredients just until a soft dough forms.

4. Gradually add ¼ cup flour, 1 tbsp at a time until right consistency is achieved.

5. Knead dough for 6 to 8 mins on lightly floured surface until smooth & pliable.

6. Place dough in bowl that is lightly oiled on the inside, cover with damp cloth, and set aside in a warm spot for dough to rise for about an hour/ until it doubles in volume.

7. Knead dough down. Roll pieces into golf ball-sizes. Arrange on floured baking sheet, cover with dish towel. Leave balls for 30 minutes until doubled in size.

8. Heat skillet over high heat and coat with light layer of oil using pastry brush/paper towel. Roll ball into circle and cook in skillet for 2 to 4 mins/ until bubbles begin and edges start to turn brown. Repeat until all balls are cooked, oiling the skillet each round. Brush tops with olive oil before serving.

Vegan Tofu Tikka Masala

Time: 55 minutes | Marinate time: 60 minutes | Serves: 4

Ingredients:

- 1x 400g (14-ounce) package firm/extra-firm Tofu
- Tofu Marinade:
- ½ x 225g (8-ounce) container Soy yogurt (vanilla/plain/lemon; reserve remnants for tikka sauce)
- 1 tbsp Lemon juice
- 1 tbsp Oil
- ½ tsp Chili powder
- ½ tsp Garam masala
- ½ tsp Turmeric
- ½ tsp Salt
- Vegan Tikka Sauce:
- 1 tbsp Olive Oil
- 1x 400g (14-ounce) can crushed tomatoes (do not drain)
- ½ tsp Paprika
- ½ tsp Cumin
- ½ x 225g (8-ounce) container Soy Yogurt

Preparation:

1. Prepare marinade by whisking together ½ a container of soy yogurt, oil, turmeric, lemon juice, garam masala, chili powder, and salt in a small bowl. Set aside.

2. To prepare the Tofu, cut tofu into bite-sized cubes. Arrange in a wide shallow pan in a single layer, and cover with marinade. Refrigerate for at least an hour.

3. Bake tofu at 175℃ (350°F) for 30 mins, turning once or twice.

4. Make the Tikka Sauce by heating 1 tbsp oil in sauté pan. Add the remaining ½ container of soy yogurt, tomatoes, cumin, paprika and any extra marinade. Heat until slightly thickened, 8 mins.

Palak Paneer (Spinach and Cottage Cheese)

Time: 40 minutes | Serves: 6-8

Ingredients:

- 500g (1 lb) Paneer, cut into 2.5cm (I-inch) cubes
- 125g (¼ lb) Fenugreek leaves
- 500g (1 lb) Spinach
- 4 tbsp Oil
- 1 large Tomato, diced
- 1 large Onion, finely chopped
- 2 tsp Garlic paste
- 2 tsp ground Coriander
- 1 tsp Ginger paste
- 1 tsp Cumin
- ½ tsp Turmeric
- 1 tsp Garam masala
- Salt
- Garnish: 1 tbsp Butter

Preparation:

1. Stir-fry the paneer in 2 tbsp oil until golden. Remove and drain on paper towels. Set aside.

2. Fry onions 2 tbsp oil until soft. Add ginger and garlic pastes and fry for 1 min.

3. Add spinach, tomato, coriander, fenugreek leaves, turmeric, cumin, garam masala and salt. Cook until spinach and fenugreek leaves are like pulp and then mash into a coarse paste.

4. Add fried paneer and coat well in the gravy.

5. Garnish with butter and serve hot with Chapatis, parathas or Roti

Sabzi Indian Mixed Vegetables Recipe

Time: 25 minutes | Serves: 6-8

Ingredients:

- ¼ cup Mustard Oil
- 1 tbsp Cumin seeds
- 2 chopped Onions
- 1 tbsp Mustard seed
- 1 tbsp Fresh Ginger, minced
- 1 tbsp Turmeric
- 1 tbsp Fresh Jalapeño, minced
- 2 tsp Coriander
- 1 tsp Garam masala
- 1 tbsp Fenugreek (optional)
- 1 chopped Cauliflower
- 1 cup Peas
- 2 cups Spinach
- 3 large Tomatoes, chopped
- 2 Bell peppers, chopped
- Pinch of Salt

Preparation:

1. Fry mustard and cumin seeds in mustard oil until they crackle.

2. Add ginger, onions, and jalapeno pepper, and fry for 4 mins. Add coriander, turmeric, and garam masala and heat for 1 min. Add cauliflower, peas, tomatoes, peppers, mushrooms, and bell peppers.

3. Cook over medium-low heat for 10 to 12 minutes, add spinach and heat to wilt. Season lightly with salt.

Vegan Indian Cauliflower Curry

Time: 35 minutes | Serves: 3

Ingredients:

- 1 ½ tsp fresh Ginger, grated
- 2 tbsp Sesame seeds
- 3 tbsp Peanuts
- 3 cloves Garlic, minced
- 1 tbsp Cumin
- 1 tsp ground Cloves
- 1 tsp Turmeric
- ½ tsp Cayenne Pepper
- 2 tbsp Water
- 1 tbsp Oil
- 2 Onions, diced
- 1 chopped Cauliflower
- 1 ½ tbsp Lemon juice

Preparation:

1. Blend together ginger, garlic, spices, sesame seeds, peanuts, and water.
2. Sautee onions in oil for 3 to 5 mins until onions turn clear.
3. Add spices mixture and cauliflower, cover and cook for 10 to 11 mins, stirring occasionally.
4. Add lemon juice. Cook for 4 mins.
5. Serve.

Quick and Easy Baked Vegetarian Samosas

Time: 35 minutes | Serves: 12-16

Ingredients:

- 2 Onions, chopped
- 1 tbsp Coriander
- 1 tsp Cumin
- ¼ tsp Cayenne pepper
- 225g (½ lb) Potatoes, cut into 2cm (½ inch) pieces
- 275g (10 oz) frozen Peas, thawed & drained
- ¼ cup fresh Coriander, chopped
- 9 sheets thawed phyllo pastry
- 2 tsp Olive oil
- Salt and pepper to taste

Preparation:

1. Preheat oven to 200°C (400°F).
2. Saute onions in oil until soft, 6 to 8 mins.
3. Add coriander, cumin, and cayenne, and cook for a minute.
4. Remove from heat, stir in potatoes, peas, and coriander leaves and season.
5. Stack ¾ phyllo sheets together, and use kitchen scissors to cut into 4 rectangles. Cut all the phyllo sheets and cover with plastic wrap.
6. Place 2/3 tbsp of potato and pea mix in corner of dough. Roll corner towards the center, fold in left and right corners, and roll up again.
7. Lightly brush samosa tops with olive oil and bake on a baking sheet, for 20 mins.
8. Serve warm.

Indian Yellow Split Pea Dal

Time: 40 minutes | Serves: 4

Ingredients:

- 1 cup raw yellow split Peas
- 2 cups Water/Vegetable broth
- 1 tsp Turmeric
- ¼ tsp Cayenne
- ½ tsp Salt
- 1 tbsp Margarine
- 1 diced onion
- 1 ½ tsp Cumin
- 2 whole Cloves
- Pinch of pepper

Preparation:

1. Simmer split peas and water or vegetable broth in a large pot.
2. Add cayenne, turmeric, and salt and cover. Cook for 19 min, stirring occasionally. For smoother texture, cook for another 20 mins.
3. Cook onion, cumin, and clove in margarine in frying pan for 4 to 6 mins.
4. Combine split peas and onion/spices mixture and simmer for 5 mins.
5. Season to taste. Serve hot.

Vegan coconut curried lentils

Time: 30 minutes | Serves: 4

Ingredients:

- ½ large chopped Onion
- 1 tbsp Oil
- 1 tsp Cumin
- 1 tbsp Curry powder
- 2 whole Cloves
- 3 cups water/vegetable broth
- 1 cup Lentils
- ¾ cup Coconut milk
- Salt
- Optional: red pepper flakes

Preparation:

1. Heat onion until soft in oil for 3 to 4 mins in a large sauté pan. Add spices (curry powder, cumin, and cloves) and sauté for another minute, stirring.

2. Reduce heat to medium-low, and add lentil and water/vegetable broth. Cover and cook for 10 to 15 minutes, stirring occasionally.

Vegan Crock Pot Curried Rice and Lentils

Time: 5 minutes | Slow cook time: 4 hours | Serves: 4

Ingredients:

- 1 cup Rice
- 1 tbsp Curry powder
- 3 ½ cups Vegetable broth
- ½ cup Lentils
- 2 vegetarian bouillon cubes
- ½ tsp Garlic powder
- ¼ tsp Pepper
- 1 Onion, dice

Preparation:

1. Combine all ingredients, stir, cover and cook for 4 to 5 hours on low.
2. Season to taste and serve.

Easy Gluten–Free and Vegan Vegetable Rice Biryani

Time: 30 minutes | Serves: 3-4

Ingredients:

- 2 tbsp. olive oil/ghee
- ½ onion, chopped
- ½ tsp Cumin seeds
- ¼ tsp Turmeric
- ¼ tsp Ginger powder
- 1 tsp Coriander

- 2 cups water/Vegetable broth
- 1 cup Basmati Rice
- ½ cup frozen Peas, thawed
- 2 to 3 tbsp Raisins
- 1 to 2 tbsp Slivered almonds

Preparation:

1. Sauté onions in olive oil over medium heat for 2 mins. Add turmeric, ginger, cumin seeds, and coriander, and toast for 1 or 2 mins.

2. Add rice and vegetable broth/water. Bring to boil, reduce heat and simmer for 15 to 20 mins until liquid is absorbed. Remove from heat, stir in thawed peas, and then raisins and almonds.

Lauki Vadi Ki Sabji

Time: 20 minutes | Serves: 4

Ingredients:

- 4 cups Bottle of Gourd, peeled and cubed
- 2 tbsp Oil
- ⅓ cup moong dal vadi
- 1 tsp Ginger paste
- ¾ cup Tomato puree
- 1/8 tsp Asafoetida
- 1 tsp Cumin seeds
- 1 tbsp Coriander powder
- ½ tsp red Chili powder
- ¼ tsp Turmeric
- 1 tsp Salt
- ¼ tsp Garam masala
- ½ cup Water

Preparation:

1. Stir-fry moong dal vadi for 1minute in oil then remove.
2. Add remaining tbsp of oil and heat cumin seeds until they crackle. Add asafetida, tomato puree, ginger, coriander powder, turmeric, salt and chili powder, stirring occasionally until oil separates.
3. Put bottle of gourd, vadies and ½ cup of water with the spice mixture into pressure cooker and cook for 6 mins. Remove from heat and release pressure.
4. Adjust the water if needed, add garam masala and serve.

Instant Pot Gajar Halwa

Time: 35 minutes | Serves: 4

Ingredients:

- 1 tbsp Butter or oil
- 3 tbsp Cashews
- 3 tbsp chopped dates/raisins/ currants
- 2.5 cups grated Carrots
- 4 tbsp Sugar

- Pinch of Salt
- ¼ cup Almond meal
- ¼ cup Milk
- ¼ tsp ground Cardamom
- Pistachios/Cashews

Preparation:

1. Sauté cashews over medium heat in butter or oil for 2-3 minutes until golden, stirring occasionally.

2. Add dates/raisins and cook.

3. Mix in carrots, sugar, almond meal and salt. Cook for 1 min and add milk.

4. Pressure cook for 7 mins and release pressure, open and add cardamom. Adjust according to taste.

5. Cook to reduce for 3 to 4 mins. Add another 2 tsp butter and mix in if required. Remove from heat and simmer for 14 mins, stirring once.

6. Garnish with chopped cashews or pistachios to serve.

Instant Pot Sweet Potato Lentil Curry

Time: 50 minutes | Serves: 4

Ingredients:

- ¾ cup Lentils soaked in warm water for 15 mins
- 1 tsp Oil
- ½ Onion, chopped
- 4 cloves Garlic, chopped
- 2.5cm (1 inch) Ginger, chopped
- ½ hot green chili, chopped
- ¼ tsp Turmeric
- ½ to 1 tsp Garam masala
- ½ tsp Cumin/ground Coriander
- 2 medium Tomatoes, chopped
- 1 cup chopped Eggplant
- 1 cup cubed Sweet Potatoes
- ¾ tsp Salt
- 2 cups water
- Large handful Spinach
- Cayenne and lemon/lime to taste
- Pepper flakes

Preparation:

1. Sauté onion, ginger, garlic, chili and salt for 2 to 3 mins. Stir often, add tomatoes and spices and cook for 4 to 6 mins.

2. Add veg, salt, lentils and water. Pressure cook on high for 11 to 12 mins. Remove from heat and allow pressure to release.

3. Open and mix in spinach, cayenne and lemon./lime. Let it rest for 2 mins and adjust consistency if required.

4. Season to taste and serve with flatbread or rice.

Eggplant Sambar – Indian Yellow Lentil Tamarind Dal

Time: 40 minutes | Serves: 4

Ingredients:

- 1 tsp Oil
- ½ tsp black Mustard seeds
- 2 dried red Chilies, optional
- ¼ tsp Fenugreek seeds, optional
- 10 coarsely chopped Curry leaves,
- 3 Cloves Garlic, chopped
- ½ cup red onion, chopped
- 1 tbsp Sambhar Powder
- 2 medium Tomatoes
- ½ tsp ground Turmeric
- 1 to 2 cups chopped Eggplant
- ½ cup chopped green Bell pepper OR ½ cup carrots
- Salt
- 1 cup split pigeon peas toor dal, washed and soaked for 16 mins & drained
- 2.5 to 4 cups Water
- 1 to 2 tsp Tamarind paste concentrate
- Cilantro and lemon grass.

Preparation:

1. Heat mustard seeds in oil in pressure cooker until they pop, 10 seconds. Add red chillies, fenugreek seeds, and curry leaves. Heat for a few secs, then add onion and garlic and cook for 5 minutes

2. Add sambhar powder and cook for 30 seconds. Add turmeric and tomatoes and cook 6 to 9 mins until tomatoes are saucy. Mix in vegetables.

3. Add split peas, salt, water and tamarind and mix well. Pressure cook for 11 to 15 mins. Remove from heat and release pressure. Open, and add tamarind extract if needed. Season to taste. Heat through.

Soup

While it is well accepted that soup was first enjoyed way back in human civilisation in Ancient Greece when the discovery was made that the nutrients from boiling meat and vegetables were released into the water, Indian cuisines embrace both clear soups and thick soups. Indian soups typically have a chicken base, shredded meat, cream, and vegetables, even fruit, and the signature Indian spices and curry. As a comfort food it is nevertheless nutritious, flavourful, and delightfully aromatic.

Soup Recipes

Chicken Shorba

Ingredients:

- 100g (3.5oz) Chicken, boneless and shredded
- 500ml (17,5oz) Chicken Stock
- 1 tbsp Garlic, Finely Chopped
- 1 tsp Cumin Seeds
- 1 tbsp White Flour
- 2 tsp Butter
- 1 tbsp Oil
- Salt & White Pepper
- 1 tbsp Fresh Cream

Preparation:

1. Fry chicken in heated butter until tender. Remove from heat and set aside
2. Cook Cumin seeds in heated oil until they splutter. Add garlic and sauté, add flour and cook for a minute.
3. Add chicken, white pepper, chicken stock, and salt and cook over medium heat for 4 min, stirring constantly.
4. Stir in cream to serve.

Hot and Sour Soup

Ingredients:

- 2 tbs chilli sauce
- ½ tbsp Corn flour
- 2 tbsp chopped spring onions
- 1 tbsp Soya sauce
- 2 tbsp vinegar
- 2 tbsp chopped Green bell pepper
- 2 tbsp chopped carrots
- ¼ cup cabbage, chopped
- Small block Paneer (optional)
- 2 tbsp tomato sauce
- ½ tsp Sugar
- Pinch Ajinomoto
- Salt & Black Pepper
- 4 cups water

Preparation:

1. Bring to boil 4 cups water, Soya sauce, chili sauce, sugar, vinegar, Ajinomoto salt, and pepper.

2. Add vegetables and cook for a minute over medium heat.

3. Stir corn starch into ½ cup water. Add to soup, stirring constantly until it thickens. Cook for 1 min. Add paneer.

4. Serve hot.

Curry Soup

Ingredients:

- 50g (2oz) Arhar dal, boiled
- 1 tsp Ginger Paste
- 1 tsp Garlic Paste
- 50g (2oz) tomato puree
- 7-8 Curry Leaves
- 3 cups Water
- ¼ tsp Turmeric
- Salt & Pepper to taste
- 2 tsp Butter
- Garnishing:
- ½ cup Boiled Rice
- Lemon

Preparation:

1. Fry curry leaves, tomato puree, ginger and. garlic paste in melted butter and add salt, turmeric powder, dal and if necessary more water. Boil.

Tamatar Ka Shorba

Ingredients:

- 600g (1.3lb) Tomatoes, washed and quartered
- 1 tbsp Chopped Ginger
- 1 tbsp Chopped Garlic
- 1 tbsp Whole garam masala
- 2 Bay leaves
- 1 tbsp chopped Coriander
- 1 tsp Cumin seeds
- 1 tbsp Sugar (optional)
- 1 tbsp Oil
- 2 Green chilies, halved
- Salt

Preparation:

1. Combine tomatoes, garlic, ginger, green chilies and Whole Garam masala to bay leaf and 5 cups water. Bring to boil and simmer for 19 mins over low heat. Strain.

2. Heat cumin seeds in heated oil in a pan until they crackle. Mix in strained tomato liquid and bring to boil and season with salt to taste, adding sugar if desired.

Daal Shorba

Ingredients:

- 4 Eggs, hard boiled and shelled
- 1 onion
- ½ pureed Tomato
- 1 / 2 green Chilies
- 3 to 4 Garlic flakes
- 1 - 2 cm (½-inch) Ginger
- Red chili powder
- 2 tbsp chopped Coriander leaves
- ¾ tsp Turmeric
- ½ tsp Coriander
- ¾ tsp Garam Masala
- 1 cup Peas OR 250g (9oz) paneer, cubed & golden fried
- 2 to 3 tbsp Ghee
- Salt

Preparation:

1. Blend garlic, onion, ginger and green chilies into a paste.
2. Heat oil in kadhi and fry onion-garlic paste.
3. Fry spices, except garam masala, for 1 min, add tomato puree. Fry until oil separates. Add cup water and reduce.
4. Add 1 cup water, fried paneer cubes or peas, and boiled eggs. Bring to boil, reduce heat and simmer for 10 mins.

Disclaimer

The opinions and ideas of the author contained in this publication are designed to educate the reader in an informative and helpful manner. While we accept that the instructions will not suit every reader, it is only to be expected that the recipes might not gel with everyone. Use the book responsibly and at your own risk. This work with all its contents, does not guarantee correctness, completion, quality or correctness of the provided information. Always check with your medical practitioner should you be unsure whether to follow a low carb eating plan. Misinformation or misprints cannot be completely eliminated. Human error is real!

Picture: YARUNIV Studio
Design Oliviapro Design

Printed in Great
Britain
by Amazon